UNDERSTANDING
EATING
DISORDERS

UPFRONT HEALTH

Published in the United States of America by Cherry Lake Publishing
Ann Arbor, Michigan
www.cherrylakepublishing.com

Reading Adviser: Marla Conn MS, Ed., Literacy specialist, Read-Ability, Inc.

Photo Credits: ©vadimguzhva/Getty Images, cover, ©TunedIn by Westend61/Shutterstock, 1, ©Hill Street Studios/Getty Images, 5, ©iStockphoto/Getty Images, 9, ©Westend61/Getty Images, 10, ©PenelopeB/Getty Images, 15, ©Thomas Barwick/Getty Images, 16, ©iStockphoto/Getty Images, 17, ©Thinkstock/Getty Images, 19, ©iStockphoto/Getty Images, 21, ©Maskot/Getty Images, 25, ©Tetra images RF/Getty Images, 27, ©iStockphoto/Getty Images, 29, ©iStockphoto/Getty Images, 30

Library of Congress Cataloging-in-Publication Data has been filed and is available at catalog.loc.gov

Cherry Lake Publishing would like to acknowledge the work of The Partnership for 21st Century Learning.
Please visit *www.p21.org* for more information.

Printed in the United States of America
Corporate Graphics

ABOUT THE AUTHOR

Renae Gilles is an author, editor, and ecologist from the Pacific Northwest. She has a bachelor's degree in humanities from Evergreen State College and a master's in biology from Eastern Washington University. Renae and her husband currently live in the Northeast with their two daughters, dog, and flock of backyard chickens.

TABLE OF CONTENTS

CHAPTER 1

A World with Eating Disorders

Food is essential to life. All animals need to eat. Humans are no exception. Yet sometimes humans have unhealthy relationships with their food. People may eat much less or much more than their bodies need. They have bad eating habits. These habits can turn into eating **disorders**.

When a person eats, their body breaks down the food. It uses the food for energy. This energy is measured in **calories**. Most calories are used to power the body's basic needs. This includes the flow of blood and the beating of the heart. Calories power physical movement, such as walking and talking. Eating more calories than the body needs leads to weight gain. This happens because the body stores unused

Binge-eating unhealthy foods has immediate and long-term consequences on the body and mind.

calories as fat. Weight loss happens from eating fewer calories than the body needs. This causes the body to burn fat instead of new calories.

Many people from the past have had unhealthy eating habits. There is evidence of eating disorders among the ancient peoples of Egypt, the Middle East, China, and Europe. Romans would **binge** during feasts. Then they would vomit so they could continue eating. Women during the Renaissance would starve themselves. It was an expression of their religious beliefs.

Who Suffers From Eating Disorders?

*There are many **stereotypes** around eating disorders. Many people think that only young, white females can have one. Studies show that as many as 4 percent of teen females have an eating disorder. It is about 2 percent for teen males. The rate is 2 percent for adult females. It is 1 percent for adult males. Research also shows rates are similar among people with different backgrounds. This includes Hispanic, African American, and Caucasian teens in the United States. What conclusions can you draw from this information?*

For hundreds of years, doctors thought eating disorders happened because of disease. They thought if a patient was sick, an eating disorder was part of their symptoms. It wasn't until the early 1900s that doctors started to see things differently. Doctors now believe that eating disorders come from complicated emotional, social, and mental troubles.

Recently, eating disorders have been on the rise. Today, as many as 30 million Americans suffer from an eating disorder. That is almost 10 percent. Men and women of all ages are affected. But the highest rates of eating disorders are among young women.

Over the course of their lives, most people go through periods of bad eating habits. It is normal to eat a lot over a holiday or skip breakfast for a few weeks. When food habits truly become a problem, they are not a lifestyle choice. They are a **mental illness** that can be deadly.

Media Influence

*The number of people with eating disorders has increased in the past 50 years. Many people say the **media** is the cause. They argue that the media focuses on men and women who are exceptionally thin and beautiful. This causes the average person to be unhappy with how they look. Studies have shown that the media makes teenagers want to lose weight. Some try dieting and exercise. Others try unhealthy eating habits. Many teenagers say they know the media makes them feel bad. How do you think the media, teenagers, and eating disorders might be related?*

CHAPTER 2

The Effects of Eating Disorders

The three most common eating disorders are anorexia, bulimia, and binge-eating. Anorexia is when someone eats fewer calories than the body needs. They do this every day for long periods of time, sometimes years. Bulimia is when someone eats more than they need and then **purges**. They purge by vomiting or taking medicine that makes them go to the bathroom. Sometimes they do a lot of exercise. Binge-eating is when someone eats many more calories than the body needs. They usually eat it all at once and do not purge.

An estimated 1 percent of young women suffer from anorexia.

Anorexia is the most deadly of all mental illnesses. People with anorexia usually have a distorted **body image**. They think they are overweight, even if they are dangerously thin. They have a fear of gaining weight. People with anorexia become very strict about their eating. They might start eating less and less. Over time, their bodies stop getting the **nutrition** they need. Anorexic people can become very sick. Their bones, muscles, and organs become weak. Their hearts and brains are damaged. Finally, their organs can start to fail, leading to death.

Bulimia affects 4.7 million females and 1.5 million males in the United States.

A person suffering from bulimia is usually of normal weight or overweight. They also have a strong fear of weight gain. People who vomit after binges hurt their bodies. This includes damage to the throat, jaw, and teeth. People with bulimia develop different stomach problems. They can get sick from not having enough water in their bodies. A lack of proper nutrition can lead to a stroke or heart attack.

Binge-eating is the most common eating disorder. People who binge-eat tend to be overweight or **obese**. When binging, they eat very quickly. They keep eating once they are full. They tend to eat in secret. They feel very bad about themselves when they are binging. Binge-eating is linked to serious illnesses, such as heart disease and diabetes. People who binge-eat might also get high blood pressure and cancer.

Effective Weight Management

*Pick up a magazine or watch TV and you are likely to come across a new diet. Most of these diets are "crash diets." Crash diets recommend eating far fewer calories than the body needs. This makes people burn fat. They lose weight quickly. Most crash diets do not work in the long-term. People gain the weight back. Improving your overall health and **fitness** is much more effective. This means good habits with food and exercise. Stress management and sleep are important too. Good health and fitness takes many years, not just a few days or weeks. What are some of your health and fitness habits? How can they be improved?*

Most people with eating disorders suffer from other mental health issues. Many have anxiety or mood disorders. Some struggle with impulse control. This means they have no control over their actions. People with eating disorders might also have problems with drugs and alcohol.

Good Eating Advice

It is not easy to eat healthy. People look for guidance on what and how much to eat. There are many organizations that give advice. They include the Centers for Disease Control and the U.S. Department of Agriculture. The American Heart Association and the American Academy of Pediatrics also put out food guides. It is common for these groups to change their recommendations. It is also common for them to not agree. Why do you think the recommendations often change and disagree? How can you choose which is right for you?

Eating Disorders

Anorexia

Eating Habits	Symptoms	Feelings	Social
few calories, limited types of food	extreme weight loss, food obsession	depression, fear, obsession with body weight and shape	won't eat with others

Bulimia

Eating Habits	Symptoms	Feelings	Social
binging and then purging	sore throat, dehydration	guilt, anxiety, obsession with body weight and shape	might eat with others, but hides binging

Binge-Eating

Eating Habits	Symptoms	Feelings	Social
binging without purging	extreme weight gain, tiredness	self-hatred, obsession with body weight and shape	hides binging from others

CHAPTER 3

Teens and Eating Disorders

Eating disorders can develop at any age. Issues with food tend to begin around 11–16 years old. Most people are **diagnosed** when they are 18–20. There is no simple reason as to why a teen might develop an eating disorder. It might be because of family history, social pressure, or emotional stress. Many people think it is a combination of all these things.

Researchers have found that eating disorders run in families. People who have a family member with an eating disorder are at least 10 times more likely to have one themselves. Teens might pick up a family member's eating habits just by being around them. New research shows it might be due to **genetics**. There might be a specific gene that makes a teenager more likely to get an eating disorder.

About half of young women in the United States think they are overweight.

The teenage years are a time of many challenges. Teenagers are trying to find out who they are and how they fit in. They receive a lot of pressure from the media and the people around them. Teens go through physical and **hormonal** changes. Their body shape might change. They might gain weight suddenly. These changes only add to the confusion about what is right for their bodies. Many doctors think anxiety and a need for control may be root causes of eating disorders. When a teen feels like their life is out of control, they start to control their body.

Teens feel pressure to look a certain way from their peers, as well as celebrities and the media.

When feeling social pressure or a need to control their bodies, a teenager might change their eating habits. They count calories and make strict rules. They set goals and obsess over reaching them. They feel guilty for eating a lot of food. So they purge. Or they hide their eating from others. Unhealthy eating behaviors can lead to an eating disorder. They might also trigger the gene that begins one.

Most people with eating disorders experience guilt and shame over their food decisions.

Airbrushing Reality

Every year, makeup companies make more than $84 billion in the United States. They make a lot of this money from people seeing their ads. For years, makeup companies have changed their photographs on the computer. They use a technique called airbrushing. A model's acne, moles, and scars are removed. Eye, hair, and skin color is changed. Even the shape of their face can be edited. In the 21st century, many makeup companies have stopped airbrushing. Others are adding labels to their ads. The label warns shoppers the photos have been airbrushed. Many of these companies have seen increased sales since making these changes. Why do you think companies are changing their methods? Do you think it will help people with body image and eating problems?

Eating disorders are some of the most common mental illnesses that affect young people. They can be very dangerous to their bodies and minds. The sooner a teenager gets help, the better. Early diagnosis means treatment can start sooner. This can stop an eating disorder from becoming deadly.

Anxiety and Control

When you are not always the one in charge, it is easy to feel like you do not have control over your own life. There are healthy ways to exercise control. One way is to practice control over your stress and emotions. If feeling anxious, stop and breathe deeply. Extra oxygen decreases the symptoms of anxiety. Then explore what thoughts led you to feeling stress. You can ask yourself questions. What triggered my anxiety? Why is it making me feel stress? What else do I know about this topic? It this truly important to me and my life? Many teens find it helpful to write their answers. You can keep a journal for regular use or to process times of stress.

People with severe eating disorders receive help
from doctors to restore a healthy weight.

CHAPTER 4

Solving Eating Disorders

Most people with an eating disorder do not seek treatment. Only about 10 percent get help. Among people with serious anorexia, up to 20 percent can die without proper treatment. Recovery is a long and difficult road, but it can save someone's life.

The first step to recovery is to get help. This starts with talking to someone. It can be a parent or other family member. Or it can be a guidance counselor or teacher. The conversation needs to feel safe and comfortable. Sometimes people do not feel comfortable talking to someone they know. They can find information in books or online first. There are also hotlines that they can call for advice. The National Eating Disorders Association can be reached at 1-800-931-2237. This type of support is free and confidential.

Therapy that includes family members has been scientifically shown to help people with eating disorders.

Treatment for an eating disorder depends on the type and how bad it is. At a minimum, a person will have counseling. Counselors work with patients to explore their eating behaviors. They try to identify what caused bad habits. Then they give their patients tools for creating a better relationship with food.

Many people with eating disorders go into **residential** treatment. At a treatment center, they work with counselors. They talk with other people who have eating disorders. Patients meet with diet and nutrition experts.

Know the Warning Signs

There are many warning signs of eating disorders. People lose control of their eating. They eat more or less than they planned. They have sudden and unhealthy rates of weight loss or weight gain. These people usually have poor body image. Even if other people tell them they are too thin, they think they are overweight. They start obsessing over their weight and food. Then they stop doing other things they like to do. In addition to yourself, it is important to be aware of other people in your life. If you think you or a loved one might have a problem, reach out for help.

They receive training on healthy eating. Residential treatment centers also address other mental health issues.

A person with a very severe eating disorder may be so sick that they have to go to a hospital first. At the hospital, doctors will work to keep their bodies stable. Once they are healthier, they might go to a residential treatment center.

After treatment, the work is not over. Someone with an eating disorder may still struggle. Times of stress may trigger old habits. Many people find being part of a group helps. Eating Disorders Anonymous (EDA) holds meetings across the country. Many hospitals and organizations have support groups too. In these groups, people share their stories. They share ways to help maintain recovery.

Eating disorders usually develop from years of unhealthy habits. It can then take years to establish new habits. **Relapse** is very common. About 40 percent of people with an eating disorder relapse. This means the majority of people do recover fully.

The Cost of Getting Help

Treatment for an eating disorder can be very expensive. The average program costs $30,000 a month. Many patients need at least three months of treatment. Then they need follow-up care with medical professionals. This can go on for years. The bills can add up to more than $100,000. Recent laws have increased insurance coverage. Most often, insurance still does not cover everything. People argue over who should pay for treatment. Some say it should be the family's responsibility. Others think insurance companies should cover everything. Or the government should help with the cost. What do you think?

CHAPTER 5

Making Healthy Choices

Everyone makes decisions about food each and every day. For some people, this can become very difficult. They become dangerously skinny or dangerously overweight. Most people find ways to stay healthy. They do so in a safe way. They make wise food choices and stay active physically. They reach a weight and fitness level that makes them feel strong, healthy, and confident.

Most eating disorders develop in the teenage years. This can be an overwhelming time, as teens go through many physical and emotional changes. Creating a good body image can help prevent dangerous eating habits. This is not easy to do. It takes effort and practice. If negative thoughts come up about your body, stop and analyze them. Replace them with positive

Stopping negative self-talk and practicing positive thinking can improve a person's health and wellbeing.

thoughts. Give appreciation for your body and what it lets you do. Keep a list of what you like about yourself. It should include your accomplishments, skills, and personality traits.

Teenagers may start bad eating habits because they feel stress or a lack of control. There are better ways to address these feelings. Try practicing control over your time. Use a planner and a calendar to track your schedule. Make daily to-do lists. These lists should prioritize your health and fitness, as well as your school and home responsibilities. Creating a relaxing environment for yourself is important.

This means turning off the TV and smartphone. Learn to be quiet and calm without distraction, and without the negative influence of the media.

When making choices, it is important to think about the effects unhealthy eating behaviors can have on your body and mind. It is important to know about the dangers and consequences of eating disorders. It is also important to think about your future. What are your priorities? What are your goals? How might they be affected by dangerous eating behaviors?

A History of Food & Nutrition

People's eating habits have changed a lot over the past 100 years. With the rise of store-bought prepared foods, people spend much less time cooking. This lets people spend more time doing other things. But prepared foods are often less nutritious. In the past, eating out was a rare treat. Today, it is much more common. Large restaurant portions can cause people to overeat. A person's diet today is much more diverse than in the past. Fruit, vegetables, and meat from around the world can be found at most grocery stores. But people are also eating more calories than ever before. Do you think these changes are for the better, or not?

[21ST CENTURY SKILLS LIBRARY]

Many experts suggest "mindful eating," which includes eating slowly, paying attention to the body's signals, and appreciating food.

Body Diversity

There are 7.6 billion people in the world, each one with a different body size and shape. This diversity can be sorted into three main body types: ectomorph, endomorph, and mesomorph. Knowing your body type can help guide you in nutrition and exercise choices. Ectomorphs are thin and tall. They might have trouble gaining weight and building muscle. Ectomorphs make good long-distance runners. Endomorphs are stocky and curvy. They have larger bones and gain weight easily. Endomorphs make great sprinters and weightlifters. Mesomorphs are somewhere in the middle. They gain weight and muscle easily. Mesomorphs do well with a variety of activities.

[21ST CENTURY SKILLS LIBRARY]

While many ectomorphs excel at running long distances,
people with all body types can learn to enjoy running.

Binge-eating was not officially recognized as its own disorder until 2013. For decades, doctors thought binge-eating was just a type of bulimia. Doctors now recognize it as a different disease. Today more people suffer from binge-eating than any other eating disorder.

Many people think binge-eating is a modern-day phenomenon. Why might they think that? Other people think it has existed for hundreds of years. It just took science a while to catch up.

What is your opinion? Use the internet or the library to further research binge-eating. Does your research back up your own ideas? Or has your opinion changed?

Learn More

BOOKS

Darpinian, Signe. *No Weigh!: A Teen's Guide to Positive Body Image, Food, and Emotional Wisdom*. Philadelphia: Jessica Kingsley Publishers, 2018.

Greene, Jessica R. *Eating Disorders: The Ultimate Teen Guide*. Lanham, MD: Rowman & Littlefield, 2014.

Lanser, Amanda. *Food Science: You Are What You Eat*. History of Science. Minneapolis: Abdo Publishing, 2015.

Mallick, Nita. *Conquering Binge Eating*. Conquering Eating Disorders. New York: Rosen Publishing, 2016.

Mara, Wil. *Body Image in the Media*. Global Citizens: Modern Media. North Mankato, MN: Cherry Lake Publishing, 2019.

ON THE WEB

Beat Eating Disorders
https://www.beateatingdisorders.org.uk/your-stories/recovery

BMI Calculator for Child and Teen
https://www.cdc.gov/healthyweight/bmi/calculator.html

GirlsHealth
https://www.girlshealth.gov/nutrition/healthy_eating/index.html

GLOSSARY

binge (BINJ) to do something a lot, such as eat, drink, or watch TV, in a short amount of time

body image (BAH-dee IM-ij) the mental picture a person has of their own body

calorie (KA-luh-ree) a unit of heat used to measure the energy food gives the human body

diagnosed (dy-ig-NOHST) given a doctor's conclusion about what is causing symptoms

disorder (dis-OR-dur) a mental or physical illness

fitness (FIT-nuhs) a person's general state of wellness and strength, but not necessarily weight

genetics (JEN-et-iks) the process of passing down qualities and characteristics, such as physical appearance and risk for disease, from parents to children

hormonal (HOR-moh-nul) having to do with the chemicals made by the body that influence the brain and bodily functions

media (MEE-dee-uh) the ways that messages are made available to large groups of people, including newspapers, TV shows, movies, and music.

mental illness (MEN-tuhl ill-NESS) a health issue with the mind, thoughts, or emotions

nutrition (noo-TRISH-uhn) the vitamins, minerals, and other necessities in food that create a healthy body

obese (oh-BEECE) extremely overweight

purge (PURJ) to rid oneself of something seen as impure or unwanted

relapse (RI-laps) to start an addiction or bad habit back up again after quitting

residential (rez-i-DEN-shuhl) requiring people to live there

stereotype (STER-ee-oh-tipe) an assumption or belief, usually overly simple or false, about other groups of people

INDEX